photograph

Also by W. R. Watkins

You. Are. Not. Alone.
An Obsessive Infatuation
Little Red Book

photograph

W. R. Watkins

First published 2018

1st Edition

Front cover art designed by W. R. Watkins

Printed and distributed by CreateSpace

ISBN 978-1-537-35828-4

Find out more at www.wrwatkins.co.uk

Mum
Dad
Clem
Fenella
All my friends
All of Team TW

This is for you x

Dear Reader,

I'm so excited to share with you my latest collection of words, 'photograph'. This is a book I've been wanting to write for a long time, and I am so happy that it is finally here. So much has happened personally since 'You. Are. Not. Alone.', that I feel this is the proper follow up to it, as well as looking at all parts of life and celebrating it for what it is, rather than what it could be.

Photographs are so important to me. They capture perfect moments in time, preserving memories, letting you look back on your life and the path that has led you to the very point you are at now. They hold so many stories, the laughter and the love that will always be cherished. Poetry, in a sense, does the same thing. They are written memories of the writer's life, who or what influenced their words, what was happening in the world, how the course of their lives changed their writing process. I most certainly can't write like I used to when I first wrote 'You. Are. Not. Alone.', 'Infatuation' etc. and that's a good thing, because it shows that I've grown as a person and, I guess, hopefully as a writer, and I hope that it is reflected in the works you're about to read.

'photograph' is such an important book to me, creatively and personally, and I hope that you enjoy coming along with me on this journey.

Happy reading!

Heartbeat

When we first heard your heartbeat,
you couldn't imagine our reaction.
The happy tears started to flow,
our dream no longer an illusion.
Your heartbeat sounded so full of life,
we began to imagine what you'd look like.
Will you have your father's nose,
will you get your mother's eyes?
Will you inherit your grandfather's wisdom,
will you have a long and happy life?
Every day we listened to your heartbeat,
looking forward to having you in our arms.
Gazing into your gorgeous eyes,
holding you close to us at long last.
Helping you to grow each day,
hearing your first words, your sweet laugh.
Doing whatever you want to do,
from science to mechanics, to history of art.
Watching you take your first steps in this world,
on a path that you'll make your own.
And all this time, giving you so much love,
that you'll never know any sorrow.
We can't wait for that approaching day,
everyday listening to your heartbeat grow.

for all the parents

"I love you Mum and Dad."

I know that I don't say it enough,
properly appreciating your love.
And I'm left feeling guilty inside,
that I don't say that often to you.

All the events you took me to,
teaching me how to swim,
and how to multiply two by two.
You picked me up when I fell down
never failing to say you were proud.
And all I want is to repay your love,
by succeeding in this difficult world.

I remember the stories you read to me,
in the funny voices, I asked for persistently.
And how you softly sang me to sleep,
telling me how much you loved me.
You held me close when I had bad dreams,
whispering how they weren't real,
protecting me in every single way.

It is a love so unconditional,
loved me more I thought possible,
and again, I don't say it enough,
I love you so much mum and dad.

"Thank you."

infinite love

Is there such a thing, as an infinite love?
Something that really has no end to it,
that transcends all you've daydreamed of?

There is your parents' love that never ends,
standing strong beside their children,
always supporting and protecting them.
They'll always love you no matter what,
they'll do all they can to be there always.

But can you find infinite love outside family,
from somebody you can give your heart to?
From someone who truly means "I love you",
is this something too good to be true?

Everybody deserves to feel infinite love.

Lend me your hand,
take me down the path.
Past the walls you've built,
to the castle that's your heart.

common ground

Others think you're difficult,
but I think you're interesting.
We're as insecure as each other,
which is helping our bonding.
We've been hurt by past love,
making us careful this time around.
Talking about everything and anything,
finding more of our common ground.

black n' white

My world used to be black n' white,
until you brought colour back to my life.
And as I lay here with you at my side,
I wonder how I ever survived alone.
Everything was monochrome, it was no life,
convincing myself I was happy inside.
You have no idea how you've changed me,
giving my life a reason to continue living.

a moment of tenderness

Come close to me
No words needed
Hold me close
This is all I need
Listen to me
Be there for me
Like I need you now
Comfort me in the way
Only you know how to
Take me far away
To that place only for us
Where I feel safe enough
To open my soul to you

midnight fire

...and as we lit the midnight fire,
and watched the flames rise,
couldn't help but wonder,
what would happen next in our lives.

...and as the embers glowed,
like the city night lights,
that you'd see on night flights,
started to reflect and think,
what will come beyond this...

When one door closes; another opens
When one life ends; another begins
After every storm; a rainbow appears
After every moment of sadness; there is joy
And when one story ends; another starts.

toys (bang bang)

Bang bang
Another one of us dead
Bang bang
Another bullet to the head

How many more should have to fall
before we realise the cold hard truth:
we're not playing with toy guns anymore?
Innocent lives being lost every day
how can we turn a blind eye to the
spreading disease of undiluted hate?

Bang bang
More lives come to an end
Bang bang
What is there to defend?

How many more deaths does it take
before realisation sinks into our society
that there must be a immediate change?
All that potential for excellence lost
the brothers and sisters now gone
unfairly forced to pay the ultimate cost

Bang bang
It's getting more intense
Bang bang
All this loss is senseless

One more father not coming home
a devastating loss to a grieving family
who now must silently suffer alone
The pleads for life falling on deaf ears
false accusations, sentencing final breaths
the effects forever rippling on for years

Bang bang
It's never in self-defence
Bang bang
Why is there never any comeuppance?

All those childhood toys
that we played with everyday
when we were young boys
It doesn't seem so much fun now
with all the lives being lost
innocent voices blocked out

Bang bang
"His hands were in the air"
Bang bang
Another friend dead

Why has progression stopped?
When was our morality lost?
Prejudice and unfounded fear runs wild
Revealing humanity's worst side
A side we once thought had died
wiped out so many years ago

Bang bang
Rest in peace
Bang.

trapped soul

When I look in the mirror,
I see a trapped soul, in the wrong body.
I try to be what they expect of me,
yet with every fibre of my inner being,
I know deep down instinctively,
that I'll never ever be truly happy.
I live in seclusion with my secret,
hiding it safely from the world.
Because I fear the judgement and hurt,
that could be hurled my way.
I dream to be free, to be who I truly am,
finally, comfortable in the skin I'm in.
But right now, I'm a trapped soul,
waiting to be freed.

teacher

Teacher, teach me my life lessons,
from the mistakes I made in the past.
Please may the lessons stay with me,
let them never again be repeated...
...unless there is more I need to learn
that I didn't learn the first time around.

Teacher, teach me to gradually accept
the parts of me I haven't learnt to love.
Everytime I see me, I don't see me,
I see the version that I love to hate.
Internally self-deprecate every part
that will permanently be out of shape.

Teacher, help me to climb the mountains,
that I think are impossible to climb.
Every step I take seems to set me back
taking me further from where I want to be,
historically never been able to achieve
anything that I've ever wanted to be.

Teacher, please hold your hand out to me,
and guide me through this twisted maze.
Show me the path you think is right for me,
lead me from the danger that is my mind.
It's been my own worst enemy for so long,
chipping away my self esteem over time.

stillness

Every morning of every day,
to let our thoughts take a break,
we need a moment of stillness.
To feel that peace that we lose,
for even just a moment of two,
whether we're aware of it or not.
Reconnecting before disconnecting,
no proper chance for recognising,
where we want our lives to be.

There is so much noise in the world,
it's difficult to let our souls be heard,
it's difficult for us to find the quiet.
So many unacknowledged experiences,
we don't appreciate their full meaning,
since we let them pass us by so quickly.
Our stillness is now so hard to find,
that some people never find it in their lives,
even though it can just be a silent prayer.

Not living in the moment here and now,
we forget how to live with ourselves,
and project out an imitation of happiness.
We need to reconnect with our souls,
to rejoin our body, mind, spirit and bones,
rediscovering whom we've become.
Letting that stillness settle into our minds,
reflecting back on what has been our life,
and giving it some space to let it all sink in.

I told you my greatest secret,
and you turned your back to me.
The one person I thought I could trust,
let me down almost dutifully.
Do you remember how you once said,
that we could tell each other anything?
How was I to know there were conditions,
to the friendship you were offering…?

no words

No words.

That's what we've been reduced to.
An uncomfortable silence between us.
No longer talking like we used to.
It's so strained that I can't stand it.
And it frustrates me you have no clue,
pretending that nothing has happened.
I find myself struggling to know what to do,
how do we move on, if we can at all?
But I believe once no words are spoken,
there's no chance for recovery at all.

excuses

"I think we should only be friends"

There they are, those familiar words.
My worst fears have been realised,
and now comes the inescapable hurt.

"It's not you, it's me"

That's what I say in return,
because I know I was difficult to love,
and we both ended up burnt.

"We'll keep in touch"

And there's the untrue truth,
we'll slowly phase the other out,
to forget what we went through.

"It's not the right time"

But maybe in another life it is,
it just wasn't our time now,
we have too many broken pieces.

seen the light

As I turn and walk away from you,
there are so many voices screaming:
"Why are you giving up again?"
"Why are you letting go so easily?"
"He promised that he would change,
maybe this time…he'll keep it."

The truth is, I'm tired of fighting,
tired of fighting for your affection,
when you readily give it to others.
Something that was once endearing,
how you paid attention to everyone,
now I see it was a distraction from me.

Now I've finally seen the light,
it was never me, it was always you.
I gave you every inch of my heart,
I even tore out my soul for you.
But you never were going to return it,
I gave everything you asked of me.

I was never going to be enough,
I finally understand that now.
So please let's part amicably,
let me out of your life peacefully.

shards of glass

I have to dig deep into my soul,
to recognise the answers I already know.
I look at the pictures that surround me,
your face the only thing standing out clearly.
Even when I smash all the frames,
it doesn't erase any of this pain.
Shards of glass are tearing up my feet,
giving me something else to feel this week.
I don't want to feel this weak
I gave you my heart, gave you all of me,
now I don't have anything left of me.
You drained all that made me up,
disguising what you gave back as true love.
Shards of glass are scattered around this room
reflecting this broken fool's dreams.

mend my broken heart

Please give me a chance
to mend my broken heart.

(Please give me a chance to breathe)

To get over the shock
that this is over before it got to start.

(I didn't want this to end this way)

I know that we were in the slow lane
but that doesn't help subside the pain.

(Told my heart that everything was fine)

Somewhere in my heart I knew
but I never listened to it.

(It was constantly present in my mind)

Because I thought this would be different…
…I thought that you would be different.

(Was I a fool to have trusted you?)

Now I feel all alone again
with my broken heart.

(I let my walls down for you)

Didn't think I'd go through this again
why does it always have to be this hard?

(I need time to mend my broken heart)

It's so hard to smile
when nothing feels right.
Everything is falling to pieces
and there's no end in sight.
You wake up in the morning,
wishing it was still night.
So that you could avoid it all,
until you're alright to smile again.

clouds

I remember the warm summer day,
when we were laying in the fields.
Gazing up at the passing clouds,
concealed from everyone else.
Painting pretty pictures in the sky,
forming the funny cloud shapes.
What you didn't know then,
was how I pretended it was a date.

We continued to gaze at the clouds,
sharing our memories together.
Laughing at our funny moments,
listening to each other's thoughts.
Letting all our secrets into the open,
consoling each other, bringing us closer,
in ways that we'd never achieved before.

Let time encapsulate that memory,
preserve the moment from fading,
not to be another story of the past.
Let's cherish the innocence of the moment,
for it to always be that special memory,
that will stay with the both us.

memories (little town)

I walk around the streets
that I love and grew up in.
Watching all the changes
to the town, I've always lived in.
All the cracks in the pavement
committed to memory.
Walking past our old hide outs
where we always used to meet.
The park that was special to us,
re-imagined for others to love.
My childhood surrounds me,
holding all the precious memories.
Those trips to ancient castles and
all the Friday afternoon visits.
Oh, it's all still so vivid,
almost as if it could be relived.
New discoveries made every day,
old lessons learnt being re-made.
Experience leading the way that
my life was going to take.
This little town has shaped me,
and all the people in it in some way.
The people I once knew as friends
still dear to me, in my memories.

rainy summer night

It's late on a summer night,
the heat is still tangibly thick,
the sound of a storm slowly rolling in.
As the raindrops begin to fall,
vivid images begin to stir back to life,
taking me back to a similar night.

I can see it all so clearly,
how you came through the crowd,
and with the first words you spoke,
you let everything I'd buried out.
You took me into the summer night,
where it had steadily begun to rain.
And in the rain, you slowly kissed me,
freeing me from my crushing anxiety.

I felt my walls coming down for you,
liberating a side of me rarely free.
All of you was intoxicating me,
silencing the tiny voice in my head,
that was saying, "Time to leave."
My heart enjoying the feeling of belonging,
and how this felt so right after so long.

As the night slowly began to wind down,
you never let me out of your sight.
I can feel the elation that I felt that night,
the same elation when I look at you now.
Lying by my side in the early hours,
years after you became the love of my life,
ever since that rainy summer night.

behind the camera

All the photographs that surround me,
have me behind the camera.
Documenting that moment in time,
for us to relive over and over again.
To keep the smiles frozen,
the happiness they held for life.
The before and after of the moment,
still replaying clearly in my mind.
An unrecorded memory movie reel,
each of us having our own editions.
But the still frames that we have,
to remind us of life's celebrations.
Never to let them get tarnished,
by whatever happened next in life.
Always better to keep memories pure,
keep all the goodness of it in our minds.
They will linger on for all of our lives,
precious moments filled with euphoria.
And to be honest, how glad am I,
to have captured them behind the camera.

A butterfly spreads its wings,
and prepares to take flight.
Patiently awaiting the moment,
to leave its old life behind.

happy oblivion

I can feel myself sinking
deep down into a happy oblivion,
that is seeping through my veins.
A sense of pure delirium,
which has no competitor,
all from simple pills and a needle,
that has become my new companion.

...

...

It takes me…so…ffar…far…away,
from all my…troubles and..doubts.
…that no one…could possibly un..understand,
…why…I continue…to seek this placce out

…the world melts into a…meaningless blur…
a colourful mixture…that has..no form
no..structure…no.rules…no..repercu..cussions
it is this…h.happy oblivion…
…that I seek…r..re…..refuge in
to essscape…all the of the re.al world's pain
..each do.dosage…getting stron...stronger.
hoping to one day..to make these visits…
…more of a..permanent vacation…

….

...

..

.

spider

I should have never met you
You spun your lies with no truth.
Knowing full well what to say and do
Manipulating what I thought of you.
Toying with your words of "pain"
Leading your support web astray.
Made me think it didn't happen that way
When you knew all this was a game.

You were a spider playing with its prey
Masquerading as the victim for sympathy.
Acting blind as if you couldn't see
Until karma got you eventually.
Now you can pay for their suffering
Reaping the pain that you caused mentally.
Just one last thing I got to say to you:
Destroying someone's life, that's on you.

monster

Many people have faced this monster before
Only a few have survived to tell the tale
No one has been able to find a cure
Some people say anything new will fail
They don't believe its reign will ever end
Evolving itself deliberately slowly over time
Robbing any dignity its victim had left.

show them

There will be times in your life,
when people will try to put you down.
Saying, "You're not good enough,
you'll never be what you've dreamt about."
Well I'm here to say to you,
you are worth more than they think.
You have the absolute potential
to fulfil every single one of your dreams.

Your self-worth is so much more
than anything they have to offer you.
Take the pain you feel in two firm hands,
let it propel you to start those plans
that you'd put aside so long ago.
Make your life that one you want to live,
not being held back by all the negatives,
you don't need to have any of it around.

Don't doubt yourself, trust yourself
and do what you feel is right for you.
If that means leaving behind somebody
who was keeping you from being somebody,
don't be afraid to have a leap of faith,
and let them be part of your history.

Show them what you're made of.
Show them what they've missed out on.
Show them how happy you are now,
and you can grow stronger without them.
Show them that your dreams can be real.
Show them who you can be.

The bumblebee does an impossible thing.
Every fact about it says it shouldn't fly.
And yet it defies nature's expectations and laws,
taking flight each day without having to try.
So, if this little humble bumblebee can do this,
then, what is stopping you taking a risk?

tumbler glass

It's 3am, I'm sitting alone
staring at your contact photo.
And I start wondering,
why did we break up again?
Why did I throw this away,
something that was so perfect,
for something that was stupid,
why did I make this mistake?

My thoughts wander in a maze,
the empty tumbler glass falling.
Been drinking every single day,
numbing the feeling of betrayal.
I want to reach out to you,
and find out how you're doing,
are you in the same place as me?

Scrolling through all our old texts,
from when we first began talking,
to when I asked you out for a date.
All the "Good morning" messages,
the quizzes we had for each other.
Through to all the cute things,
that always made me smile,

But now I'm all alone again,
battling destructive thoughts,
I caused us so much pain.
It hurts to just look at your name.

stay

I must wonder now: why did I stay?

Coming back to you repeatedly,
grasping to the hope you felt the same.
I feel so much regret looking back,
all the time that I wasted,
chasing someone so complicated,
who never knew that they hurt me.

Are you able to feel...anything?

...

...

...

...but I guess...some good came from it all,
I have a better idea of what I want now,
whether you do is no matter to me,
you missed out on somebody,
who could've loved you unconditionally.
...could've loved you so blindly

Then in a sense it was good I chose to stay,
it gave me the clarity that I needed to see,
the realisation that I can do better than this.

ruined road

I sit in the middle of the ruined road
The one you said we'd walk together
All our memoires are shattered
The ones we'd made with each other
Before me, the bricks lie upturned
Broken to pieces, mirroring my heart
Reminiscing over how you once said
"Nothing can ever break us up."

But, I will rebuild this road for us
Because I still believe in our love
Believe that we can outlast
This moment that has broken us
What we had, we can have again
So I'll rebuild this ruined road and
When you're ready, we can try again.

I'll love you at your best
I'll love you more at your worst
Only if you promise one thing:
you'll do the same in return

photograph

You look like a photograph,
not changed since I saw you last.
All the emotions still the same,
it's impossible to forget that day,
how it all played out for both of us,
how I let you slip from my grasp.

Every defining feature still there,
the eyes that let me know you cared,
the pain they held when we parted.
I feel so much regret for not telling you,
I was scared to admit I felt the same way.
Is it too late for starting over again?

Every song I hear, every story I read,
take me to when you were there for me,
sometimes I find myself wondering...
I have a photograph of us by my bed,
and I wonder where we'd be if I had instead
given you the answer we both wanted.

What would the memories of us have been?
What stories would the photographs tell?
Could we have made each other happy?
Secretly hope you're wondering as well.

bliss

All wrapped up in our little world
Holding each other so close
Not caring about anything else
Minutes and hours slipped by
Oblivious in our bubble of bliss
Kisses being stolen and gladly taken
Fingers caressing, memorising
How the other felt to the last detail
Scents and smells intoxicating
All the senses until they overflowed
Waking at dawn's early light
Watch you sleep with a smile
Bliss filling every part of me.

I never wanted to leave.

in a heartbeat

You can fall in love in a heartbeat
It can be as easy as that
You just know instantaneously
A butterfly swarm of joy
You never thought you'd feel
And it's so simple in your mind
There's no question if it's real
The connection has been made

light of my love

I know you feel that the world
has left you behind all alone.
Offering no bridge of safety,
that will bring you home to me.
Everyone else has forsaken you,
no longer returning your calls.
Leaving you in that dark place,
far from feeling safe anymore.

Let me lead you back to life,
with the light of my love for you.
Safely out the darkness in your mind,
let me be a beacon of hope for you.
Don't be afraid to tell me the truth,
that everything is not always alright.
There is no shame in vulnerability,
we all have those moments really.

You say you're crippled by fears,
I know what you're going through.
They still hold me back in many ways,
so I've been in this position too.
You're not alone in this fight anymore,
we can fight them together as one.
This is something that can be fought,
this is something that can be won.

in the future

When I think of the future
I see you and me
Being together at last
Living our life happily
It's a picture perfect moment
That I can't wait to arrive
I'm so lucky to have you
So lucky to have you in my life

wedding waltz

Take my hand in yours,
lead me onto the dancefloor,
and as the soft music plays,
let us start our wedding waltz.
Sweep me off my feet,
take us into another world,
where it is just you and me,
wrapped up in this moment,
as we dance our wedding waltz.
We look into each other's eyes,
oblivious to all the eyes upon us,
as we dance to our wedding song,
performing our wedding waltz.
Your hand pressing me close,
my hand caressing your cheek,
I'm smiling at you so happily,
you lean and kiss me sweetly,
as we dance our wedding waltz.

One more laugh

One more kiss

One more smile

One more tear

One more hour

One more day

One more memory

One more embrace

One more mistake

One more hello

One more last goodbye

…just one more with you.

simpler times

Do you remember the simpler times?
When all we had to worry about then were,
which toys were yours, which were mine?
How simplistic we thought life would've been,
when the biggest arguments we had had,
was, should we play Hide n' Seek or It?

Taking walks through bluebell woods,
going to the farm on weekends,
helping to dish out the animals' food.
Learning to ride bikes in the fields,
watching hot air balloons pass us by,
and the cushion forts we used to build.

Having sleepover with friends,
watching movies till early morning.
Playing frisbee on the Welsh beach,
having the midnight fires, and just talking.
Everything was so simple back then,
we didn't need to worry about life,
sometimes wish we could relive it again.

From Corris to the costal Borth walk,
so many memories in every corner.
Going back to bring back to life,
the memories that I lost as I got older.
Funny to tender moments flood back,
old conversations re-told over in my mind.
I don't think it's too much to say this:

"I miss those simpler times."

mark on the world

I'm going to leave my mark on the world,
make sure my voice has been heard.
Let it reverberate all throughout time,
never letting me fade from humanity's mind.
Immortalised on paper for all to read,
along with my loved ones closest to me.
Let them know that my life had meaning,
with something at the end to show for it.
Not having lived it flat until the end,
only to realise that it had been wasted.
Let them know I wanted to do good,
that I did the best that I could do.
To be the best me in this difficult world,
to make my mark on this world.

still me

I look around the darkened room,
staring at each face individually.

Where am I?

A young woman bends to my ear,
whispering that they're my family.

Who are they?

A little girl stands a little closer,
hoping for a glimpse of familiarity.

I don't know who she is

The young woman speaks again,
"This is your granddaughter."

Still nothing

Frustration begins to build,
as the memories continue to falter.

It's all slipped away

Every thin thread of memory,
slowly slipping from my grasp.

My beautiful life's tapestry nearly gone

They each take turns telling stories,
thankfully most causing them to laugh.

They're trying to rebuild what's been lost

How I used to bake cakes, throw tea parties,
teaching the grandkids all the old songs.

How wonderful my life must have been

Showing me pictures from my childhood,
of friends that have long since passed on.

I recall little of those days

The baby boy to my left gurgles,
and a small smile spreads across my face.

I know this little boy

"Samuel", I say slowly,
"Samuel is this baby boy's name".

There is a stunned silence in the room

"That's great you remember!",
says the young woman with joy.

I look back to her again

There is something familiar about her face,
the broken threads pulling back together.

The puzzle pieces are falling into place

And then the realisation dawns on me,
"You're my daughter!"

.

Everyone is crying with joy, and I am too

For the first time in what seemed eternity,
the faces and names begin to merge.

How could I have forgotten them?

But as soon as I remember,
I can feel it all start fading away again.

I can't let them give up on me

"Come close to me my dear" I whisper,
"Before you begin to fade again."

She leans in, preserving every word I say

"I'm still me somewhere inside,
even when I can't remember your name."

"So, remind me each time I forget,
tell me my life story."

"Promise me, until I remember I'm still me,
the same person you all talk about so lovingly."

***

I look around a darkened room,
staring at each face individually…

Touch is a memory
that one never forgets.
That physical presence
lingers on in the mind.
Connecting those gone
to those still living life.

the importance of faith

There are times in my life,
when the importance of faith,
has a full meaning for me.
How it can give you hope,
that everything will be okay.
It puts your worries at ease,
to have someone to confide in.
To voice all your hopes to,
and any fears you've harbouring.
It's an inexplicable experience,
to believe in more than yourself.
Having something to turn to,
when you need guidance and help.
Help to see a path that is obscured,
by the negativity before you.
Guidance to navigate it all,
and accept some difficult truths.
The importance of one's faith,
should never be underestimated.
There is a value to having one,
it provides a meaning to this existence.

lord

Lord,
Please take me in your arms.
Lay your hands upon me,
heal my broken, damaged soul.
Show me the path for me to take,
the one you set for me to walk,
the one that I have wandered from,
and now I feel lost and alone,
be my compass, guide me home.

Lord,
My heart has been broken,
and I don't have the strength,
to piece it back together again.
Teach me to understand my heart,
so I can accept someone's love,
something I don't know how to do.

Lord,
You have always been there,
even when I didn't know you were.
Been by my side all of the way,
helping my path to slowly unfurl.
My life has taken me to places,
that I never thought that it would.
I look forward to the next chapter,
and with all of my heart, I thank you.

granny nonna

a short short-story

Granny Nonna was sat in her rocking chair, taking in the warm breeze that was gently blowing down the valley. It was early autumn in the mountains, the summer flowers were slowly fading from the emerald green vista below her. The baby animals were now fully grown, and ready to set out on their own to survive and thrive. The birds, visiting for the summer, had now left to escape the coming winter, flying to the far off southern countries that she would never see, or could imagine. The mountains tops began to show the early signs of the coming weather, their pointed caps lightly covered in white that by the day slowly travelled further down, covering the rocky outcrops. Farmers living in the valley had begun to bring their livestock in. She brought the deep red, tattered shawl closer around her shoulders, protecting herself from the ever so slight breeze that travelled around her. Her ankle-length black dress, which bore the signs of age, fluttered lightly around her thin black socked ankles and her worn brown shoes, which had the worn brass buckles undone. She would have to put her summer clothing away soon, and set about stitching together the moth-created holes that had appeared in her winter clothing, which was only ever so slightly thicker that what she was currently wearing.

She gazed out over this view, watching life's work in motion.

Next to her lay her loyal black and white sheepdog, Leale. Nonna first got Leale when she was a puppy, and Nonna was a teenager. She was being sold by a farmer in the local market who had, as he said, "No use for runts." And it was true, she was on the small side, much smaller than her brothers and sisters. But she had a bright side and was smart, much smarter than the other sheepdogs that Nonna had interacted with previously. She had taken her time with Leale, training her to do her job of sheep herding right, so that if a farmer needed an extra dog, Leale would be ready to go. Ironically, a few years after getting Leale, the farmer who had sold her, was in need of extra help one winter to bring the sheep in, after one of Leale's sisters became lame, he requested Nonna's help, and he had been beyond impressed with Leale's training. Nonna had never felt prouder. Anyone who knew Nonna, knew how close she and

Leale were, one never leaving the other's side. Outside each store in the little village, was a bowl of water for Leale whenever the pair would come for their weekly shop. Nonna would always insist it wasn't necessary, but the owners were always happy to go the extra mile for her. Whilst she wouldn't admit it herself, she'd become a grandmother to everyone in that hamlet, no matter their age. They would come to her for advice or just to talk. When she was younger, she and Leale would help the farmers with their sheep, with Leale teaching the farmer's dogs a thing or two about how to do the job. The two had a connection that defied explanation, and that was beyond mere duplication. Children would often come to visit her, more so to play with Leale who was so patient with them, letting them do whatever they liked with her, within reason of course. On the very rare occasions, Leale would take herself exploring, some-times for days at a time, but always returning whenever her master called for her, even if it took her longer some days.

There had been times, when one had almost lost the other. It had been one evening many years previously, not long after Leale had assisted her previous owner with the sheep, when Leale had got her-self trapped in an abandoned mine, and had gone almost two weeks without food. When Nonna and a large team of volunteers, all the men and women in the hamlet found her, she was a mere shadow of herself. Later on, Nonna had learnt that some of the volunteers, who had remained behind in the mine to look around, had found a few recently made remains of what looked like bat skeletons. What they, and Nonna, had assumed from this discovery was that Leale had, somehow, found a way to catch bats from the nearby roost, but still had suffered severe weight loss. Nonna had stayed by her side to nurse her back to health, even though there were times that she thought she'd lose her furry friend. Ever since that episode, Nonna had noticed that whenever a bat would fly over her house, Leale would gaze after it, focused on it like a hawk, but never actually making an attempt to catch it. Another time, Nonna had suffered a bad fall in her house, breaking her hip and a few of her ribs, leaving her unable to move. Being so far away from the nearest house, if it had not been for Leale running to find someone, Nonna could well have died from the shock and the pain. And just like when Nonna cared for Leale, Leale stayed by her master's side, as volunteers came to her each day to care for her, tend to her garden, and bring anything that she needed or wanted, which for most of the time, was nothing more than the basics of survival at her own request. Earlier on, she had protested that the amount of homemade food they were bringing to her was far too much, and that they should have saved it for themselves, but they wouldn't hear of it and insisted that she should have the food.

Granny Nonna herself, had spent all her life in these mountains. She knew every peak, valley, brook and river. She knew where the juiciest berries grew; where the largest and tastiest mushrooms could be picked; how to best trap and prepare the local game, which was usually rabbit, squirrel and the odd pheasant if she was lucky. She had been an only child, her parents raising her to be the best that she could be with the limited resources that they had. But it had been a happy childhood, with lots of memories of her running through the fields, playing in the brook and climbing all the trees that were next to their house, and watching the hamlet grow into the village that it was today. This valley was her life, and she had never seen what lay beyond it. And, why should she? Every now and then, the young children would show her the latest gadget that could do things that she would never understand, nor did she need to. She would smile and sadly watch the children have such a fixation on the electronic box in their hands, until it would run out of power, and she would gently show them the beauty of her world, and would smile wider, when she would see that the electric box would lay temporarily forgotten for a few hours. She noticed that, with each passing year, the children that would visit her, were growing more and more out of touch with the wilderness around them, and whenever they brought newcomers with them, the new ones would ask what the funny furry animal with the long tail that was climbing the nearby tree was, and she would have to patiently explain to them that it was a common squirrel, which would be followed by a deep fascination with this seemingly impossible and funny creature. She'd quietly laugh when they were shocked by the size of a cow, or that the sound it made really was a "Moo!" or that the wool that made up their clothes, really did come from the funny looking clouds on legs that did nothing but eat grass each day. At times, the children would bring their parents to visit her, who in turn would bring cakes and presents for her, a luxury for her to eat such extravagant rich tasting food as a gift of thanks. Cream cakes had secretly become her favourite, with that light and frothy texture, melting as soon as it touched her tongue, followed by that burst of flavour that was woven into the mixture, which usually was vanilla.

In her youth, she was envied by the other farm girls, for having beautiful thick brown hair, that naturally went into loose curls. Her lips a natural deep shade of red and, more unusually for the people living in the hamlet at the time, dark emerald green eyes. Her cheeks were a beautiful light tint of rosie pink, with her long slender arms and legs made her figure enviable to all those who looked upon her. She had been the beauty of the valley. Now, the brown had faded to a pure white with little hints of grey breaking through, though the curls were still there, even if not as thick as they had once been. Her face, once smooth as a pearl, now bore the wisdom and experience she had gained through her years, along with the pains that came with that experience. The one thing had had never changed about her, was her smile. That same, kind-yet-innocent smile that she gave to everyone had stayed with her, drawing visitors to the hamlet in, and talking to them about whatever they wanted to talk about.

Love was something that had not been meant for her. She had the love of her parents, her friends and, of course, Leale. That was all she had ever needed and wanted. Some men had tried to pursue her, trying to win her affection, but none had ever succeeded. Being in such a remote location, young eligible men were something of a rarity, so when the last man that was similar age to her had married, a relief had flooded over her and felt the pressure of marriage lifted from her shoulders.

Now in their old age, the two lead quieter lives, with Leale rarely leaving the house without her master. Granny Nonna would spend some days tending to her little garden, watching with pride as the flowers grew and blossomed, throwing bread crumbs out for the birds, who on occasion would perch on her chair, needlessly singing for their breakfast, lunch and dinner.

Today though, in that late early autumn afternoon, there were no birds singing their songs. No children laughing or chasing each other around her garden. There was silent stillness and calm in the air, with only the gentle rustle of the conifers in the wind breaking it intermittently. A deep sense of peace had settled on the valley, one that she relished in. On her lap lay one of the latest luxury treats brought to her from the children: a small bag of sweet potato chips. She slowly ate each one, savouring the sweet taste left behind, and occasionally treated Leale to a small bite, who was always more than happy to oblige. The warm setting sun, turned the sky a mixture of blood red, pink and orange, colouring the high up clouds. The fading light, briefly illuminated her wooden house, and she closed her tired eyes to feel its warmth for one last time for that day.

The End.

let me know...

If you enjoyed this book, I would be immensely grateful if you could write a review and rate on GoodReads/your preferred online book retailer. It allows me to find out how to improve my writing, and what you thought of the book.

By leaving a review, it helps the book to become more visible to other readers, such as yourself, to discover and find this book!

Thank you so much for taking the time to read *photograph*. For further news on future book releases and giveaways, give my Facebook page a 'Like' and follow me on Twitter and Instagram.

Facebook: @AuthorWRWatkins

Twitter: @WRWATKINS2014

Instagram: @wrwatkinsofficial

about the author

Using lyrical styled writing, Watkins explores different styles of life, from the deeply explored love and romance, to topical issues around the world, to aspects of his own life.

Drawing on his own emotional responses to influence his writing, he presents a raw reflection of himself, whilst opening up and inviting readers to take part in the story he presents to them in his works.

36984843R00070

Printed in Great Britain
by Amazon